I0004978

Book 1
Open Source
By Solis Tech

&

Book 2
Human-Computer Interaction
By Solis Tech

Book 1
Open Source

By Solis Tech

Understanding Open Source From the Beginning!

Open Source: Understanding Open Source From the Beginning!

Table Of Contents

Introduction

I want to thank you and congratulate you for purchasing the book, *"Open Source: Understanding Open Source From the Beginning!"*

This book contains the basics in understanding the open source concept. What is it all about? Where did it come from? Who creates the open source content? How can software be considered as an 'open source'? What makes it different from the other software that we already have?

These questions are answered in this book. Also included in this book are information relevant to open source, such as examples of licensing, the Four Freedoms of free software use, and ideas about software piracy. This information will help to further understand what it means to have some software that is open sourced.

Real life comparisons are also made in this book in case you become confused or lost in understanding the open source concept. The idea of open source seems very simple, but in reality, it is very complex, with definitions coinciding with the definitions of other concepts such as free software (which will further be discussed in Chapter Two). Listed down in the book are the advantages and disadvantages of open source software, and the reasons why more and more people are becoming enticed with the idea of converting to open source.

If the present generation already dictates the movement of open source software, what will become of it in the future? This question is also answered in the last chapter of this book. Due to the fast-paced advancement of technology, open source will adapt to this advancement with the help of both developers and users.

Thanks again for purchasing this book, I hope you enjoy it!

Chapter 1: The Basics of Open Source

Have you ever wondered how an application you're using works? Every time you use an application and it freezes, do you think about what could have gone wrong? Do you ever think of why applications are constantly updating? These are questions that you would not be asked often. But these questions are very important to you, as a user of the Internet age.

Application programs are comprised of source codes, and these source codes are made by programmers. These codes are what allow you to type words into a word processing document, or to click on that video of cats meowing simultaneously. What you see onscreen are only visual representations of the codes of the program. Your application programs may be paid, or pre-installed in your devices, so you don't have permission to view these codes. Rather, you get the pre-made product, and you as a consumer have no power over it except to use it as instructed.

When you purchase or download an application and place it in your device, it installs a lot of files, but none of these files contain the source code. A software manager is included in your installed files to monitor the application as you use it. Whenever your application gets bugged or freezes, this software manager runs, and it prompts you to file a report to the software's developers to tell them exactly what happened. Once the report is filed, the developers study the bug, fix it, and release an update a few days or weeks later.

But what if you could see these codes for yourself? What if, whenever something goes wrong with the application, you could easily contact the developers or ask for help from other programmers easily? These questions are the foundations of open source, and you are about to learn more about it in the following chapters.

What is Open Source?

Open source is a computer program that has its source code visible to the public. The public – which we can refer to as the users – have the power to view, copy, and modify the source codes to their liking. The source code and the compiled version of the code are distributed freely to the users without fixed fees. Users of open source can pretty much do anything they like with the open source programs that they downloaded, since there are practically no restrictions.

To better understand the concept of open source software, let us use an example of recipes for comparison.

Recipes start off with someone writing them down on a piece of paper. A grandma, perhaps, has a recipe for a cake, which she writes in her recipe book. She passes on this recipe to her children, and tells them that they can use the recipe whenever they like. But, they must make sure to credit her as the original creator of the recipe.

The children recreate the recipe and whenever they are asked where the recipe is from, they would always tell that it's from grandma. One of grandma's children alters the cake recipe by adding strawberries as an extra ingredient. The grandma allows this, given that she is also permitted to use the altered recipe.

This example has the same concept with open source software.

When a programmer writes a code, compiles it into a program, and distributes both the source code and the compiled program to the users, he is giving everyone permission to access everything about the program. Users can run the program, view the code, modify if needed, compile, and redistribute the modified version of the program.

The original programmer, however, would require the users to let him use the modified versions of his program, since it is his to begin with. Aside from this certain restriction, the users of the program have the freedom to do whatever they like to do with it.

Let's go back to the example of the cake recipe. One of grandma's children, the one who added the strawberries, suggests to grandma to add the strawberries to the original recipe. The grandma thinks that this is a good idea therefore she complies and replaces her old recipe with the altered cake recipe.

In open source software, if the programmer is notified of a certain modification of a user, and it is deemed to be a modification that the software needs, then the programmer will revise his program based on that certain modification. This modification is called a patch. The user who has suggested of the modification is now coined as a contributor. This process of adapting user modification to an open source software is called upstreaming, because the modification goes back to the original code.

The concept of open source depends on the communication and collaboration between the software's developers and its users. Bug detection and fixing of open source is made easier because numerous users are working simultaneously to study the source code and to compile a modified, fixed version of the code.

With open source, it is not only the developers who are finding new ways on how the software can be improved and upgraded. The users can also contribute their ideas and knowledge in the upgrading of the software. The original developer or programmer can be called the maintainer who monitors the changes in his or her original software.

Let us then go back to the cake recipe. What if another child of grandma decides to do his own version of the cake recipe? He adds raisins to the cake recipe, and asks grandma if the raisins can be added with the strawberries in the original recipe. Grandma refuses, because she dislikes raisins. Instead of being disheartened, this child decides that he would create his own version of the recipe and share it with the people he knows.

If a certain modification makes no appeal to the developer, the one who suggested the modification may opt to make his own version of the program. This act of not patching a modification from the original program is called forking. A forked program is a certain program that alters the original program in such a way that it becomes its own program.

A forked program can be described as a chip off an old block, since it doesn't necessarily separate itself from the license of the program it originated from, although it may seem like it due to the avoidance of patching. Programmers that collaborate with open source result to forking if their modified versions of the original program are deemed unfit by the program's developer.

Nonprofit organizations are the prime developers of open source software. However, due to the freedom of customization that open source has given both users and developers, even large companies are adhering to the open source culture.

How did Open Source become popular?

During the early times of computing, software followed a protocol and design with everyone conforming to a certain cookie-cutter ideal. Software was yet to be imagined as cost-free, and the developers kept their codes to themselves. But then, during the early 90's, the idea of sharing one's code to the public became an accepted idea to most users. The concept of software being free and open sourced became a reality when, after decades, the likes of Mozilla Firefox and OpenOffice were created.

Open source rose in its ranks when developers started making open source alternatives of commercial software. These alternatives are free and can easily be downloaded from the internet, enticing most users to convert to open source. What made open source rise, however, was the idea of community. Fellow programmers could interact and communicate with each other, and even with the developers, which was unheard of during the early times of computing. People could collaborate with the developers of the software and share their insights.

Open source has also given its users the freedom to fully inspect software before they use it – an action that was impossible to do with closed source software. Users who are into coding try open source and study the code line by line.

The popularity of open source software has been anticipated due to the fact that a lot of people supported the cause. Programmers started creating open source projects to contribute to the cause, and users started to get accustomed to obtaining and downloading open source software. With volunteers signing up left and right, and organizations creating their own programs, the growth and expansion of open source software cannot be stopped anymore.

Chapter 2: History, Comparisons, and Relevance

Open source was not immediately implemented until the early 90's, where more and more people began to realize the importance of being able to share the source code of software without fees and royalties. Like any other idea, open source started out as a small thought of making software free for the public, and grew into the culture that it is today.

The History of Open Source: The Open Source Initiative

Eric Raymond, an American software developer, published an essay (turned book) entitled The Cathedral and the Bazaar in 1997. The essay speaks about two different types of software, which he labels the Cathedral and the Bazaar.

In the essay, Raymond describes the Cathedral to be the type of software in which with each release of software, the source code of the software will be available. However, with each build of the software, the certain code block that has been modified is restricted to only the developers of the software. The examples presented under the Cathedral type of software were GNU Emacs (a type of text editor) and the GNU Compiler Collection (a compiler that caters to different programming languages).

In contrast, the Bazaar is the type of software that has the Internet as the venue for their development, making the code visible to the public. The example presented under the Bazaar type of software was Linux (now a widely known computer operating system), in which Raymond coined the developer Linus Torvalds to be the creator of the Bazaar type of software.

Raymond's article became popular in 1998, getting the attention of major companies and fellow programmers. Netscape was influenced by this article, leading them to release the source codes of their internet suite called Netscape Communicator. The source code of the said internet suit was what gave birth to internet browsers such as Thunderbird and SeaMonkey. Mozilla Firefox, a popular web browser today, was also based from the source codes of Netscape Communicator.

The idea of source codes being free became widespread when Linux was developed, urging people to contribute to the open source cause. Because of the increasing popularity of Linux and similar projects, people who became interested in the cause formed the Open Source Initiative, a group whose advocacy is to tell people about the benefits of open sourcing and why it is needed in the computing world.

Open Source vs. Free Software

Most people confused open source software with free software, as the two terms share somewhat the same advocacy. With understanding, it is not that difficult to tell these two terms apart.

The difference between free software and open source software can be listed down into different points. Although they have their differences, both free software and open source software have a singular goal – to publicize source codes for the users to see.

Free software focuses mainly on the ethical aspect of the advocacy. There are certain freedoms that free software are fighting for when it comes to the use of software, which cannot be given to the users by commercial software. These are the Four Freedoms of software use according to advocates of free software:

- The freedom to use the software. This means that the user is free to use the software to his or her needs, or as instructed.

- The freedom to study the source codes of the software. Since the codes are readily available for public viewing, the user has the freedom to view and study the said codes. After he or she reviews the codes, he or she then has the freedom to do the next step.

- The freedom to modify the source codes of the software to the user's liking. If necessary, the user has the freedom to customize the source code and to create a version of the program fit for the user's specific needs.

- The freedom to share the modified, compiled source codes to the public. If the program has been modified, the user has the freedom to compile and publish the modified program for the benefit of the other users who may also have the need of the program's modification. The developer of the original program should also be given the freedom and right to use the modified version of the program.

Free software allows its users to do whatever they want with a program. If they want to modify the source code and redistribute the modified code as their own, without the consent of the original developers, then they are free to do so. If the user wishes to use the source code as the base code of a new project that they are working on, then they will not be sued. The ethical reasoning of free software simply states that there are no grave restrictions when it comes to copying, revising, and republishing the already existing software.

Open source, on the other hand, creates programs with the Four Freedoms in mind. The programs which are considered open source are made for the user's convenience and benefit. The common idea of open source is a group of people working on a single open source project, attempting to create a program that will be beneficial to them, as well as the users.

Open Source and Paid Software

Open source software did indeed come from paid software. There are countless of open source alternatives for common, commercially-sold software readily available on the internet. Some examples of this are office suites like LibreOffice and OpenOffice, which are open source alternatives for the much more popular Microsoft Office.

The reason why open source alternatives of paid software exist is mainly the cost. Users would opt to pay less, or none at all, for certain software. Why pay for software when there are free alternatives that can be downloaded from the internet easily? Open source makes it possible for users who cannot afford paid software to experience the basic and intermediate features of the software, without sacrificing the quality of the end product.

Although open source may be the overall solution for users to get a feel of certain software, there are still others who would want to obtain paid software but through illegal means. This is called software piracy, an action that is still evident despite it being illegal in most countries.

Software piracy is the act of downloading or installing a paid software illegally, either through software cracks or illegally burned CDs. The most popular way to obtain pirated software is through downloading Torrent-based software crack, in which the user can get the files through different computers almost discreetly. Since these software are pirated, installing these software requires the user to turn off his or her Internet connection before installing, to avoid being tracked.

Some paid software can be bought once, and shared with different computers or devices. All of the information regarding the sharing of paid software can be found on the software's End User License Agreement or EULA. The EULA is a splash screen shown at the start of the software's installation which contains the contract between the software's developers and the user.

The EULA may allow the user to share one copy of the software to different devices, or it may restrict the user from doing so. Once the user has violated this part of the EULA, it can then be considered as software piracy.

Something that a user should be aware of is a certain license called the GNU General Public License, the license that most open source software adhere to. The license permits the user to copy, modify, and redistribute the modified code, just as long as the source files and the original codes are still documented. This is important in understanding how and why open source software is allowed to move freely across the internet without being coined as software piracy, as compared to paid, propriety software.

With propriety or paid software, the user is buying only the license. He is not allowed to revise the code, to reverse-engineer the code, and to view the code by all means. The only thing that the user is allowed to do when he purchases propriety software is to use a copy of the software that the developer has provided. It may seem like an unfair deal to some people, because a user should be able to own something that he has paid for.

Open source software changes that idea. It gives the user the freedom to see the program's source code, letting the user know the program's 'skeletal system'. Even without paying for the software, the user gets the full potential functions of the software and not just an executable copy of it.

Importance of Open Source

Technology is rapidly changing. Experts are coming up with more ways to improve the lives of other people. It is the same with those who contribute to open source projects. Their advocacy is to create free programs that will benefit the users.

Open source is important in the evolution of quality software. With a lot of people contributing to one singular project, the software that is produced will be the best of its kind as it has been meticulously observed and reviewed by the contributors. Open source gives way for the collaborative effort of different programmers and users, with the users being secondary developers of a certain program. It is an interactive effort, with the users being able to update the program alongside the developers themselves.

The fast paced advancement of technology would often overwhelm content creators to the point that they would stop creating content altogether. Content creators who are left behind by technology's advancement are often working in small groups or on their own, and have no means of help from fellow creators of their kind.

With Open source, this is never the case. Each open source software has its own community to back a fellow programmer up during each build, ready to help out other programmers and users when needed. The open source community's bond with each other is what makes open source catch up with the fast advancement of technology.

Chapter 3: The Benefits and the Downsides of Open Source

The Benefits of Open Source

The most obvious perk of having open source software is the availability of the source code. With the source code available to the general public, people are able to study the code line by line. Students of programming can study the source code and implement some blocks of it into their own projects, honing their skills and improving their code. Users who are meticulous with their software can view the codes and customize the said codes to their liking.

Aside from the source codes being publicized, another perk of having open source software is that it is mostly free, depending on the software's license. Users of open source software do not have to pay a large sum of money to be able to enjoy the full functions of the software. If the license requires the user to pay, the user may still try out the software's full functions before purchasing.

Open source promotes community. If a user encounters a problem with the downloaded software, he or she can seek help from fellow programmers or the developers themselves through a forum. Users and programmers alike can communicate and share their experiences with using the software, helping other users to get used to the software. With other programmers keen on editing and revising the source code, updated and better versions of the software can easily be uploaded and shared within the community for the benefit of the other users.

Also, when something goes wrong with the open source software, the user has the option to fix the problem himself should seeking help be an option that is not convenient for him. In propriety software, this cannot be possible as the license and copyright prohibits its users from ever touching the program's source code.

If the user of propriety software does as much as reverse-engineer the product, then they could be violating the program's copyright and therefore, be taken to jail. Open source software removes this restriction from the users, giving them permission to fix solvable program problems on their own.

The benefits of open source software are not limited to personal use. Companies and businesses are adhering to the open source paradigm due to the endless possibilities at half the price or lesser.

More and more businesses are converting to open source mainly because it is more cost-efficient than purchasing commercial software. Companies also have more freedom with open source software in terms of customization, since they have the power to mold the software to fit their company's needs. These factors are beneficial in the growth and development of businesses in such a way that the businesses need not to put out a large sum of money just to be able to acquire a software that will be utilized in their business.

Open sourcing has become a way for people to have access to the things that they initially did not have access to. Users of software now have the ability to study the source code of the program they are using, and to know how exactly a certain function of the program runs by looking at its specific line of code.

A sense of community is also created between the software's developers and programmers from outside of their firms. Through open sourcing, the developers are able to communicate with other programmers with regards to how the software can be enhanced further.

Some users would say that using open source operating systems grants more security as compared to paid operating systems. For example, if a user installs the Linux operating system, he or she does not need an antivirus or a virus detection software to keep his or her files intact. The operating system itself has security measures for the user. This becomes a benefit for both professional and nonprofessional users because they have more room for important files rather than installing different kinds of applications for protection.

Open source software is made for the people, by the people. It hones itself to the needs and wants of each user. Because of this, there is no need for the user to upgrade his or her hardware every time the software upgrades.

Take Apple's OSX (operating system) for example. Certain updates of the operating system are available to download, with better features than the previous build. However, older versions of the Macbook and the iMac cannot avail of the recent builds as their hardware are not fit enough to accommodate either the size of the downloaded file or the features itself.

With open source software, the upgrades can be coded to fit each user's needs, depending on the user's hardware. If a certain upstreamed version of the open source software is available to download, different downloaders are made available by the developer with the specifications listed beside each downloader, catering to the different specifications of the user. The user himself can opt to customize the code of the program to be compatible with his device.

Allowing the user these freedoms over the software has given open source software a bit of a leverage over paid, propriety software. But then again, there will be nay-sayers who think that open source software isn't the way to go.

The Downsides and Disadvantages of Open Source

Open sourcing has given users lots of benefits, but it is not perfect. Some would still prefer paid software over any open sourced software. Here are some of the reasons why some users do not approve of open source.

If a user is not in any way a technology expert, he or she would want software that is easy to use. Open source software is known to be more technical compared to their paid counterparts. Paid software focuses on its user interface, making the application easy for the user to understand the system. Open source software usually start out with a not so attractive user interface, but with the basic functions of the program intact. As the program gets updated with each build, the user interface changes and adapts to the needs of its users.

Most critics would say that paid or propriety software is still better in a number of factors as compared to open source software. Because more people are accustomed to using paid or propriety software, the idea that there are other types of software available is intimidating to them. People think that open source software is made only for the technology savvy users, with the interface hard for them to manipulate. Why download a complicated software when they can buy a simple, pre-made software that they are already familiar with?

Paid software has become a norm in the everyday lives of users. Large companies such as Microsoft and Apple have made their name known all throughout the world, creating technologies that users and consumers have grown to love. Because of their undying popularity, the rise of open source software is unknown to the general public. And even if they are known, those who are used to seeing the big names are hesitant to try out what open source might be.

Seeking technical help might seem simple with the numerous open source communities readily available, but it may sometimes be inconvenient to the user. Paid software offer professional tech support straight from the manufacturers.

Chapter 4: The Open Source Culture

Open source gives the user freedom to do whatever he or she wants in a software. Who wouldn't want the freedom to edit source codes to their own liking? With open source, this opportunity of customization is available at hand.

Why are more people converting to open source?

With the source code open for public scrutiny, looking for errors will be easier. Other software companies that do not have their source code publicized have their own set of programmers and developers figuring out the bugs in the software. This is an advantage for companies who always require their software to be updated regularly to keep up with the business.

Students who cannot afford the luxury of paid software turn to their open source counterparts to be able to utilize their functions without having to pay a large amount of money. Open source alternatives of Microsoft Office are available for the students to download should they need to use an office suite for their projects.

Some open source versions of paid software are actually better. Paid media players can play certain file types and extensions, but crash once the file extension is unrecognizable. Open source software developers take note of these bugs and create a media player that can play almost all media file types and extensions in high definition. Because of this, even users who are not actually technology savvy would convert to the open source alternatives of paid software just because they've heard and they know that they can get more out of the open source counterpart.

Programmers who want to practice their coding also rely on readily available open source software in their study. Because the codes of open source can easily be viewed and modified, programmers can base their project on open source software and publish it as their own, creating a program fork.

Businesses, on the other hand, turn to open source software for two main factors: cost efficiency and the power of customization. As mentioned in a previous chapter, with open source software readily available to download on the internet, the businesses do not need to spend a lot of money for a software that they cannot customize as their own. Open source gives them the opportunity to keep on upgrading their system as needed, therefore improving the quality of their software with each build.

The flexibility of open source software has enticed businesses to change to open source from propriety software. Businesses would often buy already existing software and attempt to use them as instructed by the developers. Open source software has its own rules and regulations, but if businesses want their software to be something specific, then the developers of open source software will deliver. With propriety software, the business is the one to adjust to the software that they have purchased, an action that is removed once businesses convert to open source.

Examples of Open Source Software

A wide variety of open source software are available for download. These software may be used for utility purposes, for multimedia purposes – anything that the user desires and requires. Here are a few examples of open source software that you as a user have probably heard of.

The prime example of open source software is an operating system called Linux. It is an operating system based off of UNIX that is available to different computer platforms and hardware.

Another example of open source software is the media player called VLC Media Player developed by the VideoLAN Organization. This media player can run a variety of multimedia files at high definition. Its paid counterpart is Microsoft's own Windows Media Player, which before its most recent build can only play a handful of file extensions.

When it comes to operating systems, Android is another popular example of open source software. A company called Android, Inc. (later bought by Google) has developed this mobile operating system using another open source kernel, Linux. It caters mostly to devices which have touchscreen on them, such as touchscreen desktop monitors, tablets, and smartphones, much like its counterpart from Apple called iOS. Android has its own application store called Google Play, where the users can install applications onto their phones mostly for free.

Netbeans, a well-known software developing application, is also an example of an open source software. It is a Java-created application that caters to different programming languages, and can be run on multiple operating systems. Programmers use Netbeans to create object oriented applications using the 24 programming languages that it caters to.

GIMP, or GNU Image Manipulation Program, is an Adobe Photoshop-like application that edits photos and creates graphic images. It has basic photo editing features such as cropping, grayscaling, and resizing, making it a simpler alternative to Photoshop. Like its paid counterpart, users of GIMP can also create animated GIF images, a feature that most multimedia artists are very fond of using.

Video and computer games can also be open sourced. Some open source games such as Tux Racer are available in the Linux package when downloaded. The principle of open source games is the same as any other open source software – the developers merging and collaborating with the users to create quality content to be distributed to the general public. However, the visual quality and elements of open source games are yet to be improved.

Other examples include PHP (a web development language), MySQL (used in databases alongside applications such as Microsoft Access and Microsoft Visual Basic), Python (programming language), Blender (an Autocad Maya-esque application that caters to 3D rendering), and many more.

Chapter 5: The Future of Open Source

What will happen in the future?

The future of open sourcing seems bright. With most businesses converting to open source software and most developers contributing to open source projects, the growth and expansion of open sourcing will continue. Open sourcing gives way for the innovation of modern software technology – with a lot of people working on one simple open source project, there is no doubt that the project will continue to be updated and improved.

Software will only continue to improve as time passes by. Open source software has made it easier for software to improve and upgrade itself due to countless of volunteers who are up to the challenge. While propriety software claim to start software trends, open source software advocates the upgrades of software that will be favorable to the needs of the users rather than to the bank accounts of the developers.

Open source software does not wish to waste the time and money of the user; rather, it aims to maximize both time and money, with the inclusion of effort, of the user when utilizing the software.

Presently, paid software are still dominant over open source software. Paid software have more leverage compared to open source software when it comes to reliability and familiarity, since they have been used by programmers and users alike for decades. There is still a certain percentage of users who are not aware that there are open source versions of their paid software, which they can help improve and customize to their own needs and liking.

More people will be aware of the benefits of open source software in the future. With propriety software releasing more licenses that restrict its users from certain software freedom, the existence of open source will lead to the users converting from propriety software due to the lack of free will.

In the future, there is a possibility that open source will be available not just for software, but also for other forms of content that have sources.

The future of open source as an idea or a paradigm will not be restricted to software alone. With the further advancement of technology, more and more gadgets will be locked down by licenses and warranties which restrict its users from fixing even simple problems that the product may have.

Gadgets are becoming more and more digitized, and copyright restricts people from ever touching or attempting to change the software. Because of this, some people are beginning to open up to the idea of open source not just for software, but also for hardware and gadgets that are used every day.

Let us take tractors for example. Tractors are machines that are essential in farming. If a tractor breaks down, the farmer himself can fix the broken tractor and keep it running again without having to buy a new one. But the modernization of technology leads the manufacturers of tractors to add digital aspects into their products: tractors now have microchips and are operated via computers, therefore are now protected by copyright.

Now, if the new tractor breaks down, the farmer has no permission to fix the tractor himself. He must hire a specialist to fix the problem, or else he goes to jail.

Open source hardware has already started to rise in its ranks alongside open source software. It basically means that users are free to create their gadgets from scratch, using open source hardware. Although the idea seems taboo at present, the fact that gadgets are also being restricted from the users will give way for both open source hardware and software to rise even further, giving users complete freedom over the creation and implementation of the technology that they need.

Content creators are restricted from creating certain things just because of copyright laws. Even artists, who upload videos on websites like YouTube and Vimeo, get flagged just because of a certain song or a certain speech that had some sort of copyright over it. This restricts creative freedom. It also restricts the content creators from creating what they know and love, and sharing it with their viewers.

Will open sourcing become a culture in the future? Surely, with the massive amounts of information available for the users to share freely amongst themselves. Open source software has given way for an idea that will change the world of computing for everyone, and allows everyone to have access to the large chunk of information that was previously not available to them. Transparency when it comes to creating code and building machines will become a fad in the future, as more and more people are willing and able to create content and share it with other users.

Conclusion

Thank you again for purchasing this book!

I hope this book was able to help you to understand better the concept of open source and its benefits to the public.

Finally, if you enjoyed this book, please take the time to share your thoughts and post a review on Amazon. It'd be greatly appreciated!

Thank you and good luck!

Book 2

Human-Computer Interaction

By Solis Tech

The Fundamentals Made Easy!

.

Table of Contents

Introduction

I want to thank you and congratulate you for purchasing the book, "Human-Computer Interaction: The Fundamentals Made Easy!"

This book contains proven steps and strategies on how to conceptualize and design a computer system that incorporate principles on effective interaction between the user and the device.

Human-computer interaction (HCI) is the study of the interaction between people and computers and the degree at which computers are developed enough to successfully interact with humans. So many institutions particularly academic and corporations now study HCI. Unfortunately, ease-of-use has not been a priority to most computer systems developer. The issue continues to bedevil the HCI community as accusations still abound that computer makers are still indifferent and are not making enough effort to make truly user-friendly products.

On the other hand, the designing task of computer system developers is not simple either as computers are very complex products. It is also true that the demand for use of computers have grown by leaps and bounds outstripping the need for ease-of-use by a significant margin. If you are a computer designer or simply have basic interest in making devices more effective for users, this book will help you a lot.

Thanks again for purchasing this book, I hope you enjoy it!

Chapter 1: Aspects of HCI

Main aspects of HCI

HCI is composed of three main features, namely: the user, the computer, and their interaction or how they work together.

"User" refers to either the individual or the group of users doing things together. An understanding of how the people's sense of sight, hearing, and touch send information is very important. Also, the type of mental models of interactions differs according to the personality of the user. And finally, interactions are also influenced by cultural and national differences.

"Computer," on the other hand, pertains to all technology from desktop to huge computer systems. As an example, if the topic is website design, the computer would then be the website. "Computers" would also include gadgets like mobile phones or even VCRs.

Finally, the "Interaction" is what happens as "User" uses the "Computer" to achieve a certain objective. Humans, of course, are totally different from machines. So the HCI's main intent is to ensure a successful interaction between the two.

In this aspect, adequate knowledge about humans and computers are critical to realize a functioning system. You need to seek inputs from users. Such knowledge would provide much needed information in determining schedule and budget that are crucial to the systems. In effect there are ideal situations and perfect systems. But the key is finding the balance between what is ideal and what is really feasible given the existing situation.

Objectives of HCI

HCI aims to come up with systems that are functional, usable, and safe. Developing computer systems with excellent usability depends on:

- having enough understanding of the aspects that lead people to use technology in certain ways
- being able to devise tools and ways for creating suitable systems
- the development of safe, effective, and efficient interaction

- making people the priority

The main philosophy underneath HCI is that the users or the people using the computers always come first. Developers must always be guided by the users' needs and preferences in designing systems. It is the system that should match the requirements of human users and not people changing to suit the nature of the machines.

The primacy of usability

Usability is one of the principal considerations in HCI. It is simply about ensuring that a system can be easily learned and used or be what is called user-friendly. A system is considered usable if it:

- can be learned easily
- can be remembered easily in terms of use
- is effective
- is efficient
- is safe
- is enjoyable

Lack of usability means wasted time, mistakes, and disappointments. Unfortunately, a lot of existing systems and devices have been designed without sufficient attention to usability. These include ATM, the Web, computer, printer, mobile phone, personal organizer, coffee machine, remote control, soft drink machine, ticket machine, photocopier, stereo, watch, video game, library information systems, and calculator.

A good example is the photocopier. If you are not familiar with the symbols on the buttons you will be greatly confused. For instance, the big button with the C on it actually refers to Clear, not Copy. The button used to produce copies is actually on the left side with an unrelated symbol. Devices and gadgets should be easy, effortless, and enjoyable to use.

Analyzing and designing a system based on HCI principles involve a lot of factors that produce really complex analysis because of interactions among many of them. The major factors are:

- The User – motivation, satisfaction, experience, enjoyment, personality. Also cognitive processes and capabilities

- User Interface – navigation, output devices, icons, commands, input devices, graphics, dialogue structures, user support, use of color, multimedia, natural language
- Environmental Factors – health and safety, noise, heating, lighting, ventilation
- Organization Factors – job design, work organization, training, roles, politics
- Task Factors – task allocation, skills, easy, novel, complex, monitoring
- Comfort Factors – seating, layout, equipment
- Constraints – budgets, buildings, cost, equipment, timescales, staff
- Productivity Factors – decrease costs, increase quality, increase innovation, increase output, decrease errors
- System Functionality – software, hardware, application

There are different disciplines representing a wide array of subjects that are covered in HCI. The manifold inputs from these fields have continued to enrich HCI. The disciplines include:

- Cognitive Psychology – limitations, performance predictions, information processing, cooperative working, capabilities
- Ergonomics – display readability, hardware design
- Computer Science – graphics, software design, prototyping tools, technology, User Interface Management Systems (UIMS) and User Interface Development Environments (UIDE)
- Social Psychology – social and organizational structures
- Engineering and Design – engineering principles, graphic designs
- Linguistics – natural language interfaces
- Philosophy, Sociology, and Anthropology – computer supported cooperative work (CSCW)
- Artificial Intelligence – intelligent software

Chapter 2: The Human Side in the HCI

Some of the key aspects that shed light on the human side of HCI are:

1. Perceptual-Motor Interaction. Effective human-computer interface design requires an appreciation of the whole human perceptual-motor system. The information-processing approach is central to the perceptual-motor behavior study and for considering the human factors in HCI. An effective interface design reflects the designer's knowledge of the perceptual such as visual displays, use of sound, and graphics. Also the cognitive exemplified by conceptual models and desktop metaphors as well as motoric constraints like ergonomic keyboards of the human perpetual-motor system.

   Man has gone beyond the use of computer punch cards and command-line interfaces. We now use speech recognition, eye-gaze control, and graphical user interfaces. The importance of various perceptual, cognitive, and motor constraints of the human system is now better recognized in HCI. An effective interface must take into account the perceptual and action expectations of users, the action that is seen with a response location, and the mapping of the perceptual-motor workspaces.

2. Human Information Processing. Aspects of human information processing such as models, theories, and methods are currently well developed. The available knowhow in this field is broadly useful to HCI in general such as in the representation and communication of knowledge and visual display design. An effective HCI requires making the interaction compatible with the human information-processing capabilities. Many things about human information processing have been integrated into cognitive architectures that are now applicable to HCI. These applications include the Model Human Processor, the Act model, the SOAR model, and the Epic model.

3. Mental Models in Human–Computer Interaction. Studying mental models can help understand HCI by inspecting the processes by which such models impact behavior. For example, mental models of machines can enable both novice and seasoned problem solvers to find new methods for fulfilling a task through more elaborate encoding of remembered methods.

   The Reverse Polish Notation is a great example of this. There is also a general theory that says readers develop a representation in their mind at several levels of what they read. First is the encoding of text, followed by the representation of propositional content of text. Finally, to this text, they integrate world knowledge to form a mental model of the situation described.

Readers also have the ability to look for ideas in multiple texts. They construct a kind of structured mental maps that show which documents contained which ideas even when they did not expect to need it while reading. Mental models are generally considered as semantic knowledge. Focusing on the degree of commonality among team members, for instance, when it comes to knowledge and beliefs, allows quantitative measures of similarity and differences which is the language of computers.

4. Emotion in Human–Computer Interaction. Emotion used to be persona non grata in the field of computer design. It had no place in the efficiency and rationality of computers which were the personification of zero emotion. Recent study findings in the field of psychology and technology show in a totally different light the relationship between humans, computers, and emotions.

   Emotion has ceased to be considered only in light of anger generated by inexplicable computer crashes or hyper excitement caused by video games. Nowadays, it is widely accepted that a host of emotions are important part of computer-related activities such as Web search, sending an email, online shopping, and playing computer games. In almost everything now, the emotional systems get engaged according to psychologists.

   Studies and discussions on emotion and computers have grown a lot because of dramatic advances in technology. Computers have actually been used to evaluate the relationship between emotion and its correlates. In the same vein, the astounding improvements in quality and speed of signal processing now enable computers to form conclusion on a user's emotional condition. Compared to purely textual interfaces that have very limited range, the multimodal interfaces that can use voices, faces, and bodies are now more capable to a broader range of emotions.

   Nowadays, the performance of an interface will be seriously impeded without considering the user's emotional state. Surprisingly, it can earn even descriptions like socially inept, incompetent, and cold. Much remains to be done to successfully incorporate emotion recognition into interfaces. Still, more studies about the interaction between design and testing can help create interfaces that are efficient and effective while providing satisfaction and enjoyment.

5. Cognitive Architecture. A cognitive architecture is a computer simulation program that makes use of human cognition principle based on human experimental data. It also refers to software artifacts developed by computer programmers. Likewise, the term also includes large software systems which are considered hard to develop and maintain.

Right now, cognitive architectures are not widely utilized by HCI practitioners. Nevertheless, it is quite relevant as an engineering field to usability and has important applications in computing systems especially in HCI. It also serves as theoretical science in human computer interaction studies. Finally, cognitive architectures combine artificial intelligence methods and knowledge with data and principles from cognitive psychology.

Presently-known cognitive architectures are undergoing improvements and are being utilized in HCI-related tasks. Two of the most well-known systems, EPIC and ACT, are production systems or built around one. All systems have production rules which differ from architecture to architecture. The difference lies on focus and history although there's a certain similarity in intellectual history. They may have more congruence than differences at some levels either because of mutual borrowings or due to the convergence of the science. The third system, Soar, is a bit different than the first two production system models.

The three production systems, Soar, Epic, and ACT-R were developed to present different types of human cognition but showed more similarities than divergence as they developed. It is not easy to describe a value possessed by architecture as advantage because to others it constitutes a disadvantage. For instance, Soar's learning mechanism is very important for modeling the improvement of users for a period of time. But there are many applications also where Soar's features result to harmful side effects that can cause more difficulty in model construction.

6. Task Loading and Stress in HCI. Stress in the form of task loading is central to HCI. The traditional perspective on stress sees it in light of exposure to some adverse environmental situations such as noise and the focus of attention centers on most affected physiological system. A new way of looking at it, however, stems from the findings that all stress effects are mediated through the brain.

   And since the brain is mainly focused on ongoing behavior or current task, stress ceases to be a peripheral issue but that the ongoing task becomes the primary source of stress. And this renders stress concerns that are central to all HCI issues. This means computer-based systems which aim at helping people lessen cognitive workload and task complexity actually impose more burdens and stress on them.

   The person's coping mechanism for such stress affects their work performance and personal wellbeing. The environment may vary but some mechanisms for appraising stress in all task demands are the same. So for HCI, certain principles and designs for stress are applicable across multiple domains.

There are several theories of stress and performance and their connection to human-computer interaction. Workload and stress are at times considered as varying perspectives on the same problem. There are some general practices for stress mitigation. But quite important for this topic is setting up effective measures of information processing and mental resources. It also includes expounding on task dimensions that are relevant and their relationship to self-regulatory mechanisms.

It is critical to establish how an individual's appraisal of his/her environment can be influenced by personal traits and states. This is because stress can only be understood vis-a-vis interaction between a person and the environment. Lastly, it is better to treat stress at multiple levels whether physiological or organizational when making practical application. Instead of one-dimensional which is bound to fail, multidimensional is better as it considers the person, task, and the physical, social and organizational environments.

The implication is that HCI researchers and practitioners should go beyond the design of interface displays and controls and focus also on the person aspects. What are the things in the individual that affect performance and the physical-social environment where the human-technology interaction happens? It means that the technical principles at work in that situation are not adequate. They cannot develop a complete description of the relationship between resources and cognitive activities.

7. Motivating, Influencing, and Persuading Users. From its former role as tool for scientists, the spread of computer use to all sectors of society has brought new uses for computers. Among those uses are persuading people to change their attitudes and behavior. Nowadays, it is widely accepted that skills in motivating and persuading people are necessary for developing a successful HCI.

   Interaction designers are actually agents of influence which unfortunately they have not yet understood and applied. Yet their works often involve creating something that tries to change people though they may not be conscious of it. Among these works are motivating people to register the software, learn an online application, or have product loyalty. Changing people's attitudes is now a common feature in the success of interactive products.

   Depending on the types of product, the persuasion factor can either be small or large. At any rate, anything that needs to be marketed needs to be persuasive. The growing use of computing products and the limitless scalability of software makes interaction designers one of the best potential change agents in the future.

Take for example the Web-interaction designers who increasingly are facing more challenge in designing something that will hold the attention and motivation of information seekers. After that, they need to persuade web users to adopt certain behaviors like:

- using a software
- joining a survey
- clicking on the ads
- returning often after bookmarking a site
- buying things online
- releasing personal information
- forming an online community

Being able to persuade people is a measure of success here. But with success comes responsibility. The Web designer needs to make the website credible. The following are some broad guidelines to ensure credibility:

1. Design websites to present the real and practical aspects of the organization.
2. Invest sufficiently in visual design
3. Make websites that people can easily use.
4. Include markers of good quality
5. Use markers of reliability.
6. Avoid too much commercialism on a website
7. Adopt and adjust to the user experience
8. Avoid being amateurish

To sum it all, computer systems have become an inescapable part of everyday life. The interactive experience involving all systems be it mobile phone or desktop can be designed in such a way as to influence the way we think and act. By combining the computing capability with persuasion psychology, computer systems can motivate and persuade. Humans are undoubtedly still superior when it comes to influencing people. But in many areas of endeavor, computer can do what humans cannot even imagine being capable of.

Computers don't sleep and can be designed to keep trying on and on. At the very least, computers provide a new way for modifying how people act and think. Like it or not, the community of HCI professionals is at the forefront of the campaign to make more sensitive and responsive tech products. It can rise to the challenge of helping churn out products that enhance the people's over-all quality of life. Or it can continue being a tool to produce mindless products whose main reason for being into is to make profit for the owners.

8. <u>Human-Error Identification in Human–Computer Interaction</u>. The leap from focusing on human error in technological problems to a less obvious culprit started in the 1940's. It was established during that year that plane pilot error was often designer error. It began to show that design is the key to

substantially reduce human error and this paradigm continued to gather steam particularly in HCI.

It is now common wisdom that human error can be as often as the product of a defective design or as a person making a mistake. The inadequate design fosters activities that lead to errors. A groundbreaking outcome of this new philosophy is that errors are now viewed as totally predictable events instead of seeing it as unpredictable occurrences. This makes errors avoidable.

So errors became instances where planned series of steps and activities fail to realize intended results independent of any outside change agencies. If errors are no longer random, then it can be identified and predicted ahead of time. What partially drove this line of thinking are the accidents that happened in the nuclear industry that is hungry for preemptive solutions. This has led to the formulation of several human-error identification (HEI) techniques.

Although evaluative and summative in nature, these HEI techniques that employ ergonomics methods can now be used in formative design stages especially in analytic prototyping. For instance, the entry of computer-aided design such as in architecture has profound impacts on prototyping. It made possible what was considered as impossible or too prohibitively costly design alteration at the structural prototyping stage.

The three main forms of prototyping human interfaces have been identified namely: functional analysis, scenario analysis, and structural analysis.

Functional analysis includes consideration of the functional range supported by the device. In comparison, scenario analysis is exemplified by consideration of the device in relation to events sequence. An example of the structural analysis, on the other hand, is the use of user-centered viewpoint in a non-destructive testing of the interface.

One compelling example of the crucial role of design in predicting and minimizing errors concern human error identification (HEI) tools like the TAFEI or Task Analysis for Error Identification. The results of the application of TAFEI on interface project designs show how it can improve systems and its relevance to other ergonomic methods. It served to validate what has been long suspected when it comes to error-design relationship as follow:

- Structured systems like TAFEI results to reliable and trustworthy error data;
- Most errors resulting from technology are totally predictable;

- To improve design and reduce errors, ergonomics methods should be employed in formative design process.

Exploring design weaknesses through tools like TAFEI will go a long way in developing and producing devices and gadgets that are tolerant to error.

Chapter 3: The Computer Side in the HCI

The salient points when it comes to the computer side in HCI include:

1. Input Technologies and Techniques. Input devices which are also a classification of computer can detect physical aspects of places, things, and, of course, people. However, its function is never complete without considering the visual feedback corresponding to the input. It is like using a writing instrument without something to write on. Input and output should always go together.

   And in devices with small screens, this is only possible with the help of integrated sensors. If the user or human characteristics are important in a maximized HCI environment, so are input technologies with enough sophistication to meet user-machine interaction requirements. Users can only achieve the task objectives by combining the right feedback with inputs. In this regard, the HCI designer should take into account the following:

a. the industrial and ergonomic design of the gadget

b. the physical censor

c. the relationship among all interaction techniques

Input gadgets have many properties that apply to the usual pointing devices or mobile items with touch input. These pointing devices include the: mice, trackballs, isometric joysticks, isotonic joysticks, indirect tablets, touchpads, touchscreens, and pen-operated devices. The mice or mouse, of course, is one of the most popular as anyone who has ever used a computer knows. Because of its inherent advantages for individual users where it can easily be used by most people, it is one of the most preferred pointing devices.

Touchpads are most well-known to laptop users. These are small tablets that are sensitive to touch and which are usually featured on laptop units. Touchscreens on the other hand are tablets that are sensitive to touch which are placed on a display. It is increasingly becoming the tool to beat because of the proliferation of smart phones and other hand-held devices.

There are input models and theories that are quite helpful in evaluating the efficacy of interaction strategies. But it would be most beneficial to readers here to focus on current and future trends for this feature. Interactive system designers should go beyond the usual things like graphical user interface and pointing ideas when it comes to inputs.

They must delve deeper into more effective search strategies, sensor inputs for new data types, and techniques of synthesis to make much better sense of data. Better search tools will enhance navigation and manual search regarding file systems. One outstanding development is the breakthrough in the development of more advanced sensor inputs such as technologies for tagging and location.

It allows computers to identify physical objects and locations that have been tagged, and to detect their location and distance to other devices through signal strength analysis. These sensors are making interface personalization much easier. This development in interaction also has great implications for data mining and techniques for machine learning. Continuous improvement in structure synthesis and extraction techniques is invaluable in this data-rich era.

An overriding aim in HCI is to achieve dramatic advancement in humanity's interaction with technology. The computer side of this presents limitless possibilities but the cognitive skills and senses of man will be relatively stagnant. Our holding, touching, and object-movement are not the result of technology-like progress but a product of our human limitations.

2. Recognition- and Sensor-Based Input for Interaction. Computers are able to manipulate physical signals that have been transformed by sensors into electrical signals. Sensors have found their way into various fields of industry such as robotics, automotive, and aerospace. It has also found vast applications in consumer products.

   The computer mouse is a very good example. Imagine that simple-looking device equipped with algorithms that process images and specialized camera that enables it to be unbelievably sensitive to motions. It detects movement at the rate of a thousand of an inch several thousand times per second. Another interesting device is the accelerometer that detects acceleration due to movement and continuous acceleration because of gravity.

   Digital cameras now make use of accelerometers to save a photo. Laptops also are equipped with accelerometers for self-protection. When the laptop is accidentally dropped the accelerometer enables the hard disk to secure the hard drive prior to impact. With smartphones, the goal is for motion sensing for the purpose of interaction such as determining the walking pattern of users. Generally, HCI research on sensors dwells on its usage to improve interaction.

   Sensor studies are either to broaden input options or build new computing forms. The new forms include mobile devices that recognize locations and places that are sensitive to the presence and needs of its inhabitants. Still there are far more advanced goals and applications like in robotics.

There is a race to develop machines that will behave and think like humans or at least complement their capabilities. It has many critical applications such as in nuclear power accident mitigation. One worry, of course, is that it will end up in the military. But in safety, mobile computing, entertainment, productivity, affective computing, and surveillance, sensors are finding widespread application.

An intriguing side note here is the idea of developing a sensor to enable computers to detect and accordingly react to the frustration of its user. The computer's response could be something like playing relaxing music. Sensing could be in the form of the user banging on the keyboard in frustration. A microphone could react to the yelling of the speaker or the webcam could sense scowling.

In general, the potential of interactive sensing is quite good. The degree of progress across the whole computing spectrum actually gives the impression that sky is the limit. Advances in nanotechnology, CPU power, and storage capacities will continue to produce more outstanding innovations in the computer side of HCI.

But what is driving the unprecedented growth of the sensor-based interactive systems is the dizzying expansion in devices outside the old desktop computer. It is hard to keep track of the explosive proliferation of smart phones, tablet PCs, portable gaming devices, music and movie players, living room-centric computers, and personal digital assistants. Computing is becoming part and parcel of our daily life and our environment.

Through recognition techniques and sensing systems, task-specific computing devices will be developed instead of general functions. It will also pave the way for different types of interaction style in HCI. This activity-specific interactive systems development will further hasten innovations on a much broader array of practical applications.

3. Visual Displays. Timekeeping has always been one function that man has strived for a good visual display. Today's smartwatches which are actually wrist computers sport stunning visual displays. It is no longer limited to displaying time but is multifunctional. Some brands can pinpoint exact location in the planet through a global positioning system. Others can show heart rate while a number can be personal digital assistants.

   The main idea behind wearable computing is that the human body is wearing the visual displays. One major way people use wearables is to put the display on one's head making user's hands free to work. It is called headmounted displays or HMDs. The screen-based is one category of HMDs. It makes use of the retinal-projection method which projects images on the retina of the eye.

An alternative method is the scanning displays which scan images onto the retina pixel by pixel. A second type of display which is actually much bigger in scope and the most widespread is the hand-held and wrist-worn displays. They are in mobile phones, media players, wristwatches, and other portable gadgets. Apple is one of the global leaders in this field and the most well-known. Even textiles for clothing are now being used for such technology in what is now known as photonic textiles-fabric.

Multicolored lighting systems were merged with the fabrics for its electronic information function without affecting the cloth's softness. It has sensors, GSM, and Bluetooth! Photonic fabrics have great promising applications in the areas of personal health care and communication.

4. <u>Haptic Interfaces</u>. Haptic interface refers to a device for sending feedback that produces sensation of weight, touch, rigidity, and other aspects through the skin and muscle. This force feedback mechanism is designed to enhance computer-human interaction. Because haptics are done through actual physical contact, they are not easy to synthesize unlike the sense of sight and sound that are gathered through the eyes and ears.

   The genius in the haptic interface is that it simply makes use of the body's own highly sophisticated receptor system. The haptic feedback is made possible through synthetic stimulation in the skin and proprioception.

   Proprioception involves something deeper than the skin – the muscle and skeleton. The mechanoreceptors in the body enable its detection of contact forces received from the environment. Body receptors sense velocity, skin stretching, vibration, and edges of objects. Haptic interfaces are more widely applied in the field of virtual reality than in information media and related devices are now available commercially.

Two of the most important research needs on haptic interfaces in the future concern the psychology in haptics and safety considerations. Safety is a crucial issue as insufficient actuator control can lead to injuries for users. Control problems may occur with the tool displays and exoskeleton. Unintended forces or vibration may pose danger to the user.

A locomotion interface that holds a user's body can cause serious physical damage if control is inadequate. It requires proven safety equipment that amply protects the walker and this should be a major objective of research. A much safer alternative is a system where the user does not wear any equipment during the interaction.

The psychology in haptics on the other hand requires more studies on muscle sensation as most existing findings are on skin sensation. Among the few promising findings relate to Laderman and Klatzky's work (1987) on force display and their recent study of forces distributed according to space. Their psychological findings have very promising applications in the development of haptic interface. A lot of obstacles need to be overcome before usage of haptic interface becomes widespread.

Though men cannot do without haptics in real life interaction, it is still of limited use in HCI. One can say haptic interface is still in infancy with its 10-year background. So eventually its time will come just like image displays (e.g. TV and movies) which started 100 years ago. For now, what are available are a few haptic interfaces with limited functionality and high cost. At the very least, haptic interface is a new very promising frontier in HCI with immense potential contribution to man's quality of life.

5. Non-speech Auditory Output. Sound is one of the key aspects that complete our interaction with our environment. But where speech is direct and necessitates focus and attention, non-speech sound is more diffused and provides a different class of information.

   Non-speech sounds include sounds from the environment, music, and sound effects. Nevertheless, speech and non-speech sounds complement each other just like text is complemented by visual symbols. Non-speech sounds can give information in a shorter period of time than speech.

   Right now, the non-speech field needs more research. The user interface is a much more effective tool for HCI when it employs a combined visual and sound feedback. This sound-visual combination has complementary function as well. Visual gives specific information about a small area reached by our eyes but sound or the auditory system provides more general information from beyond our focus.

   Our senses are the key to our effective interaction with the external world. These senses in turn bring more dimensions in information as they enhance one another. These principles are very useful in a multimodal HCI by adding non-speech sound output to the graphical displays. An example of this application is focusing our eyes on one task like editing a manuscript while monitoring other aspects in the machine through sound.

Reliance on visual sense which is more prevalent at present can be problematic. One problem is there could be visual overload which means the user could miss lots of information. Or simply that the viewer cannot look at everything at the same time at all times. Sound can help eliminate that situation by giving information to the user that the eyes could not see.

This interdependence between visual and audio could make information presentation far more efficient. Non-speech sound is mainly used in games' sound effects, music, and other multimedia usages. It is commonly employed in creating a certain mood for the item like in movies. In HCI, sound is used to provide information particularly those things that a user does not see or notice such as what is going on in their computer systems.

It is useful to use non-speech sound in HCI for many reasons. Seeing and hearing in the human body is first of all interdependent. The eyes can give information that is high-resolution only in a limited area of focus. But sounds can be received from all sides of the user: front, above, below, and behind. This not only provides direct information but also tells the eyes where to look to get more useful data. In fact, at times reaction to sound stimuli is faster than what is seen.

Non-speech sound can therefore help in reducing large display overload which can cause users to miss important data. This is especially true in large graphical interfaces that use multiple monitors. Using sound to present some information would reduce screen space. It would also lessen the volume of information that should be on the screen. This is most relevant to gadgets with small visual displays like smartphones and PDAs.

Non-speech sound would also decrease demands on our visual attention. For instance, a user who is walking would miss much information as he looks at his device's visual display because of competing attention from the traffic or uneven surface where he is walking. In fact, if the information is in sound, he does not have to look at his device at all.

Our sense of sound is also underutilized. Yet as exemplified by classical music, its intricate organization can make, say a symphony, a powerful tool for transmitting complex information. The beauty with sound is that it grabs attention. It is easy to avoid looking at something but hard to ignore sound which makes it very effective in sending important information. Likewise, certain things in the interface look more natural in sound than in sight.

Finally, non-speech sound will allow visually-impaired users to use computers. Newer graphical displays have, in particular, made it even harder for them to operate the device. Research has been extensive in the HCI application of non-speech sound in a wide range of topics.

There are two main areas of growth where the application of non-speech sound has the best potential. One is in the creation of multimodal displays that utilizes all available senses. This means integrating sound with other things like force-feedback and tactile apart from sight. The other area is in wearable and mobile computing gadgets that also use multimodal displays.

As mentioned, the screens of these devices are small and sound will reduce the need for screen space.

6. Network-Based Interaction. Networked interfaces have modified our perception of society and the world at large particularly with the Web and now mobile devices. There are several roles that networks play in HCI. The first is as an Enabler which refers to things that can be done only with network. The second is as Mediator which pertains to problems and issues caused by networks.

   Third is as Subject which focuses on managing and understanding networks and fourth as Platform which dwells on interface architectures and algorithms. Network includes both the wire-based and the wireless world. Things are rapidly changing especially in the wireless networks. These changes can be classified in two dimensions, namely:

- **Global vs. Local** – refers to the distance by space between the connected points such as machines in the office to global networks like the Internet.

- **Fixed vs. Flexible** – pertains to the nature of the links between points such as fixed devices and gadget that configures itself. More changes are coming because of spreading wireless links. One example is being able to gain access to internet connections and printers of another office by simply plugging a portable device into the Ethernet.

Traditionally, LANs belong to local-fixed category while Internet is global-fixed. Hand-helds like cell phones are also categorized as global-fixed because phones are fixed and independent of location. The internet makes use of domain names which are fixed like URLs. Some phone technologies like GSM and GPRS are classified as global-fixed because it is possible to send content that is based on location. Also the enlarging data capability is enabling services to handle huge media content.

What set these technologies apart, however, are the connectivity model and the charging which are usually by data use or fixed charge. There are a number of current and new technologies from the local-flexible type. These include the Wi-Fi, infrared, Bluetooth, and ZigBee which permit flexible connections among personal gadgets. With them, a computer device can utilize a mobile-phone modem or a headset with Bluetooth can make connections with a phone, wireless. Unfortunately, these capabilities also enhance unsavory activities like illegal equipment accessing, hacking, and surveillance.

7. Wearable Computers. Computers have become like appendage to many office workers. But it is hard for those using mobile devices to get the information

they need. In a mobile situation, existing interfaces will hamper the user's main task. Users will be forced to prioritize the device instead of the environment. The need is for a wearables design that helps fulfill not obstruct the task.

A framework that can be very useful in creating good designs of computer interfaces which are wearable is CAMP. This framework addresses different factors that may impinge on the effectiveness of the design such as body closeness and how it is used. CAMP stands for:

- Corporal – which means absence of discomfort to users during physical interface with the wearable.
- Attention – interface design should allow user to focus both on the real world and virtual reality.
- Manipulation – there are adequate controls which are easy to manipulate particularly in a mobile environment.
- Perception – Design must enable user to quickly perceive displays even when mobile. So displays should be easy to navigate and simple.

Outside offices and buildings, an attractive option for a user to have access to a computer interface is through wearables. There are challenges however that need to be addressed to fulfill the tasks in terms of contextual awareness, interface, adaptation to tasks, and cognitive model. These include:

- **Modalities of Input/output** – the ease of use and accuracy of modalities developed that try to copy the human brain's input/output capacity are not yet satisfactory. Frustrations bedevil users when there are inaccuracies. Also the computing requirement of these modalities is way beyond what low-weight wearable devices have. Input devices which are simple to use are needed.

- **Models of User interface** – there is a need for extensive experimentation in using applications involving end-users.

- **Capability-applications matching** – evaluation and design of interface should prioritize development of most effective way to access information and avoid creating additional features.

- **Simple methodology in interface evaluation** – current evaluation approaches are too complicated and time-consuming making them unsuitable in interface design. What is needed is an evaluation methodology that addresses frustration and human errors.

- **Context awareness** – for context aware computing to be realized, several questions must be answered. These include application models that integrate the social and cognitive aspects, social and cognitive mapping of inputs from many sensors, anticipating the needs of users, and interacting with the users.

Conclusion

Thank you again for purchasing this book!

I hope this book was able to help you to gain useful knowledge and understanding about human-computer interaction.

The next step is to apply what you have learned.

Finally, if you enjoyed this book, please take the time to share your thoughts and post a review on Amazon. It'd be greatly appreciated!

Thank you and good luck!

www.ingramcontent.com/pod-product-compliance
Lightning Source LLC
Chambersburg PA
CBHW060931050326
40689CB00013B/3046
* 9 7 8 1 5 2 3 8 6 6 7 3 1 *